DISCOVER AMERICA

UTAH

Janice Parker

AV² provides enriched content that supplements and complements this book. Weigl's AV² books strive to create inspired learning and engage young minds in a total learning experience.

Your AV² Media Enhanced books come alive with...

Audio
Listen to sections of the book read aloud.

Key Words
Study vocabulary, and complete a matching word activity.

Video
Watch informative video clips.

Quizzes
Test your knowledge.

Embedded Weblinks
Gain additional information for research.

Slide Show
View images and captions, and prepare a presentation.

Try This!
Complete activities and hands-on experiments.

... and much, much more!

Go to **www.av2books.com**, and enter this book's unique code.

BOOK CODE

P 3 5 8 9 7 4

AV² by Weigl brings you media enhanced books that support active learning.

Published by AV² by Weigl
350 5th Avenue, 59th Floor
New York, NY 10118
Website: www.av2books.com

Library of Congress Cataloging-in-Publication Data
Names: Parker, Janice, author.
Title: Utah : the Beehive State / Janice Parker.
Description: New York, NY : AV2 by Weigl, [2016] | Series: Discover America |
 Includes index.
Identifiers: LCCN 2015048032 (print) | LCCN 2015048338 (ebook) | ISBN
 9781489649508 (hard cover : alk. paper) | ISBN 9781489649515 (soft cover :
 alk. paper) | ISBN 9781489649522 (Multi-User eBook)
Subjects: LCSH: Utah--Juvenile literature.
Classification: LCC F826.3 .P373 2016 (print) | LCC F826.3 (ebook) | DDC 979.2--dc23
LC record available at http://lccn.loc.gov/2015048032

Printed in the United States of America, in Brainerd, Minnesota
1 2 3 4 5 6 7 8 9 20 19 18 17 16

082016
210716

Project Coordinator Heather Kissock
Art Director Terry Paulhus

Photo Credits
Every reasonable effort has been made to trace ownership and to obtain permission to reprint copyright material. The publisher would be pleased to have any errors or omissions brought to their attention so that they may be corrected in subsequent printings. The publisher acknowledges Getty Images, iStock Images, Alamy, and Dreamstime as its primary image suppliers for this title.

UTAH

Contents

STATE TREE
Blue Spruce

STATE BIRD
California Gull

STATE FLOWER
Sego Lily

STATE FLAG
Utah

STATE FRUIT
Cherry

STATE SEAL
Utah

Nicknames
The Beehive State

Motto
Industry

Song
"Utah, This is the Place"
by Sam and Gary Francis

Population
(2010 Census) 2,763,885
Ranked 34th state

Entered the Union
January 4, 1896, as the 45th state

Capital
Salt Lake City

Discover Utah

Utah is located in the mountain region of the west-central United States. The state's unique terrain includes snowcapped mountains, sparkling lakes, deep valleys, barren salt flats, and remote deserts. Utah also has a rugged plateau region, which features multicolored canyons and impressive rock formations. Utah's varied landscape makes it a great place for recreational activities. The state has 5 national parks, 2 national recreation areas, several national monuments, and 45 state parks. Many Utahans enjoy activities such as boating, swimming, fishing, hiking, and skiing. Most of the state receives very little rainfall, which means people can be outdoors enjoying these activities many days of the year.

Visitors to Utah will be amazed by the state's wealth of historical spots. At This is the Place Heritage Park, people can experience a historic village that re-creates life in a typical Utah community of the mid-1800s. This park remembers the many people who have called Utah home over the years. Early residents of the region that became Utah include Native Americans, Spanish explorers, Mormon pioneers, and mountain men.

Salt Lake City is the state's largest city and the state's business center. Park City is a tourist destination for winter sport enthusiasts. Today, the total area of farmland in Utah is relatively small, yet it is productive. Hay, corn, barley, and wheat are the state's main crops, but livestock and livestock products earn Utah farmers the most money.

The Land

With **4.5 billion tons of salt**, the Great Salt Lake is four to eight times saltier than the ocean.

Rainbow Bridge is the largest natural rock span in the world. It is **278 feet wide** and **309 feet high**.

Delicate Arch stands 65 feet tall and is the most iconic rock formation in Arches National Park. The park was created in 1929, but Delicate Arch was not part of it until 1938 when the park was expanded.

Mormon settlers flooded into Utah during the 1840s determined to turn the arid landscape into a fertile and productive home.

Beginnings

Spanish explorers were the first Europeans to set food in present-day Utah. In 1776, Franciscan friars traveled much of the west, spreading Christianity. It was not until the early 1800s that more people made their way into Utah. Fur traders searching for beaver are responsible for naming many of Utah's natural features.

In 1847, the first wave of Mormons arrived seeking freedom from religious **persecution**. They built homes and churches, and also established towns. In just three years, Utah gained territorial status. In the 1860s, non-Mormon settlers began to arrive seeking precious metals. By 1900, so many people had migrated to the state that the population had nearly reached a quarter million people.

In Utah's early years, mining and farming were key economic activities, and this is still the case. The economy of Utah really started to flourish during and after World War II. Defense, the steel industry, and oil refining all added financial security to the state and contributed to job growth.

Where is
UTAH?

Several other states share a border with Utah. Its neighbors are Idaho and Wyoming to the north, Arizona to the south, Colorado and Wyoming to the east, and Nevada to the west. At the southeast corner of Utah is the Four Corners, the only place in the United States where four state boundaries meet at one point. Arizona, Colorado, and New Mexico are the other Four Corners states. Utah ranks 12th among the states in land area.

NEVADA

United States Map

Utah

Alaska   Hawai'i

MAP LEGEND
- ◼ Utah
- ☆ Capital City
- ● Major City
- 🌿 Zion National Park
- ▲ The Wave
- ◻ Bordering States

① Salt Lake City

Utah's state capital is home to more than 190,000 residents. Salt Lake City was founded in 1847 and has been the state capital since Utah became a state in 1896. Visitors can experience the Natural History Museum of Utah and the Hogle Zoo. Guided tours of the city are also available, including a scavenger hunt.

② Zion National Park

Zion National Park features a **diverse** landscape in the heart of canyon country. Encompassing 229 square miles, visitors can experience high plateaus, narrow sandstone canyons, and the Virgin River flowing through the area. The park's climate diversity allows for more than 1,000 different types of plants and 67 species of mammals.

WYOMING

COLORADO

① Salt Lake City ● Park City

④

UTAH

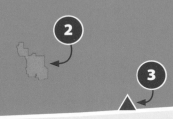

N

SCALE 0 —— 50 miles

③ **The Wave**

The Wave is located in the Coyote Buttes in southern Utah. It is a rock formation with many layers made of wind-blown sand that resemble a rolling wave. Due to The Wave's popularity, only 20 visitors are allowed each day. Foot traffic requires a special permit assigned four months in advance.

④ **Park City**

Once a historic silver mining town, Park City is now a premier winter sport destination. Located in the Wasatch Mountains, the Utah Olympic Park surrounds the city, and there are three major ski areas within city limits. Those visiting during the summer can ride on a 4,000-foot alpine roller coaster at Park City Mountain Resort.

Land Features

Utah is made up of three land regions. They are the Middle Rocky Mountains, the Basin and Range Province, and the Colorado Plateau. The Rocky Mountains occupy the northeastern part of Utah. Uinta and Wasatch are the major mountain ranges in this area. The western third of the state lies in the part of the Basin and Range Province called the Great Basin. This area contains Utah's Great Salt Lake Desert. The Colorado Plateau, in the southeastern part of Utah, covers roughly half of the state. The Colorado River winds through this region, flowing by colorful canyons, arches, and natural bridges.

Bridal Veil Falls

Bridal Veil Falls, a waterfall in Provo Canyon in northern Utah, is more than 600 feet tall.

Colorado Plateau

The Colorado Plateau is centered in the Four Corners region of the United States. Its total land area is 130,000 square miles.

Great Salt Lake

The Great Salt Lake is the saltiest lake in North America. Very few living creatures can survive in its waters.

Monument Valley

Monument Valley is located in the southern part of the state. It is known for its large sandstone formations, which have provided a backdrop to many Western movies.

Climate

Utah's climate differs from region to region. Most of the state enjoys hot, dry summers and mild winters. The average July high temperature in Utah ranges from about 85° Fahrenheit in the mountains to 90°F in the southern part of the state. January high temperatures drop to around 40°F in the south and a chilly 30°F in the mountains. The Great Salt Lake Desert receives less than 5 inches of precipitation per year. The mountain areas, on the other hand, can receive about 40 inches of precipitation each year.

Average Annual Precipitation Across Utah

The average annual precipitation varies for different areas across Utah. How does location affect the amount of precipitation an area receives?

LEGEND
Average Annual Precipitation (in inches) 1961–1990

200 – 100.1

100 – 25.1

25 – 5 and less

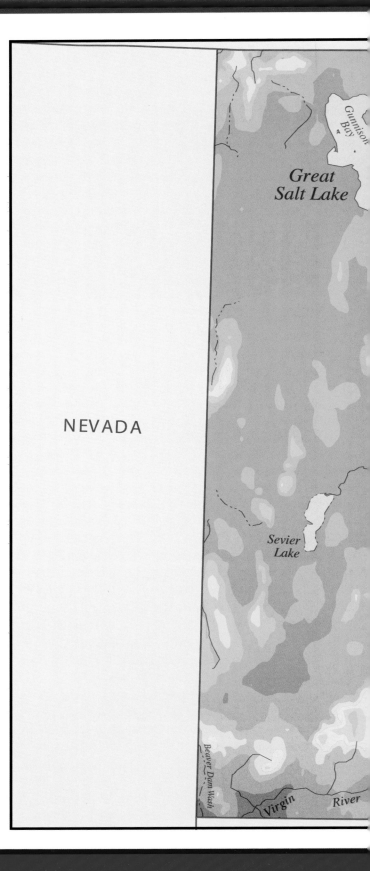

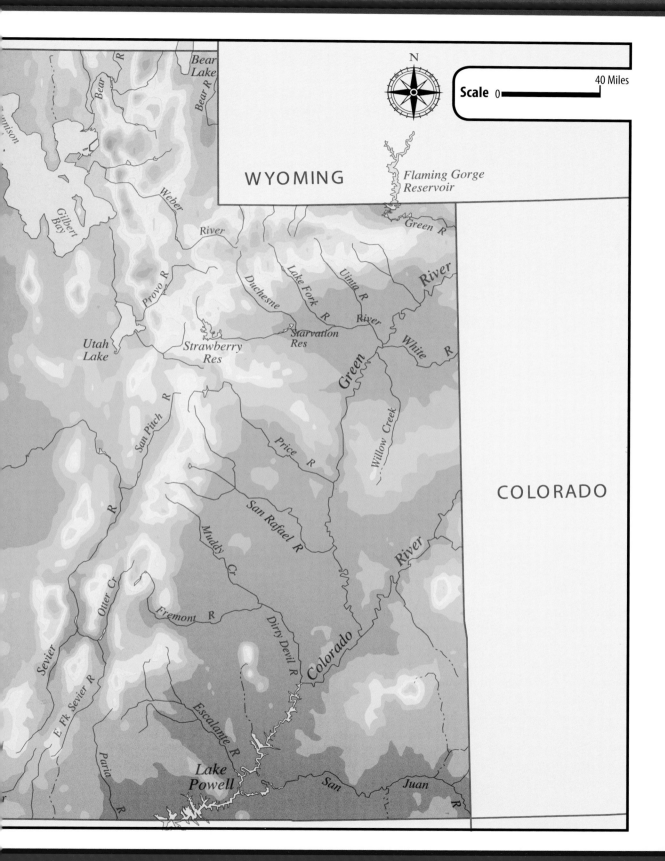

N

Scale 0 ▬▬▬ 40 Miles

Bear
Lake

Bear R

Bear R

WYOMING

Flaming Gorge
Reservoir

Gilbert
Bay

Weber

River

Green R

Provo R

Duchesne

Lake Fork R

Uinta R

River

River

Green R

Utah
Lake

Strawberry
Res

Starvation
Res

White R

San Pitch R

Green

Willow Creek

Price R

COLORADO

R

San Rafael R

River

Muddy Cr

Otter Cr

Fremont R

Sevier

Dirty Devil R

Colorado

E Fk Sevier R

Escalante R

Paria R

Lake
Powell

San

Juan

R

Utah's Bingham Canyon mine has produced more copper than any other mine in the world.

Nature's Resources

Utah is rich in mineral deposits. The state is a leading producer of copper, most of which is mined in Bingham Canyon. Gold and silver are also mined in Utah. In fact, Utah is one of the nation's leading gold producers. Iron is mined in the southern part of the state. Natural gas, petroleum, and coal are found in the Colorado Plateau. Salt and other minerals are obtained from the Great Salt Lake.

Utah is the only state that produces gilsonite, which is a mineral used in road oil and asphalt tile. Gilsonite has been produced in Utah since the 1880s. Clay, limestone, and gravel are also important to the state.

Soil is another valuable natural resource in Utah. The soil supports many crops, such as hay, wheat, and barley. In addition, much of the land is suitable for grazing livestock.

Gilsonite is a naturally occurring form of asphalt.

Utah produces more than 2 trillion tons of salt each year.

There are 18,200 farms in Utah, covering 11 million acres of land.

Vegetation

There are many forests in Utah. Trees common to the area include firs, pines, aspens, maples, poplars, Utah oaks, and willows, as well as the state tree, the blue spruce. Cacti grow in desert areas. Wildflowers, including the yucca and the Indian paintbrush, flourish throughout the state.

Flowering plants bloom during the spring and summer in the state's desert regions. At higher elevations in the mountains, strong winds and a short growing season prevent trees from growing to full height. At the highest elevations, only grasses and **annuals** grow.

Beavertail Cactus

Many types of cacti grow in Utah, including the beavertail cactus, which gets its name from its resemblance to a beaver's tail.

Indian Paintbrush

The colorful Indian paintbrush, which can be yellow, red, orange, or cream colored, grows best in areas with sandy soil.

Sego Lily

Bulbs of the sego lily were a source of food for Utah's early settlers. This lily was adopted as the state flower in 1911.

Sagebrush

Sagebrush, a common shrub in Utah, has a strong smell that discourages animals from eating it.

Wildlife

Many large mammals inhabit Utah. American black bears, mule deer, mountain lions, elk, and pronghorns live in various parts of the state. Porcupines and raccoons are common sights in the forests. Utah's desert animals include wild horses, coyotes, Gila monsters, rattlesnakes, and kangaroo rats. Some desert animals remain in their dens or burrows during the middle of the day when temperatures are at their highest. Several animals native to Utah are **endangered**, including the black-footed ferret and the gray wolf.

Bird-watchers in Utah can spot great horned owls, roadrunners, hummingbirds, and red-tailed hawks in the desert. The state is also home to numerous game birds, including the ring-necked pheasant, the ruffed grouse, and Gambel's quail. There are many eagles and hawks in Utah. Hawkwatch International, an organization created to protect **birds of prey** and their environment, has its headquarters in Salt Lake City.

Gambel's Quail

The Gambel's quail, also known as the desert quail or Arizona quail, can be found in the southern part of the state.

Utah Prairie Dog

The Utah prairie dog is listed as a threatened species. It does not live in any other part of the world.

Porcupine

The porcupine can be found in many different habitats but prefers **coniferous** and mixed forest areas.

Gila Monster

The only venomous lizard native to the United States, the Gila monster, can be found in the southwestern corner of Utah.

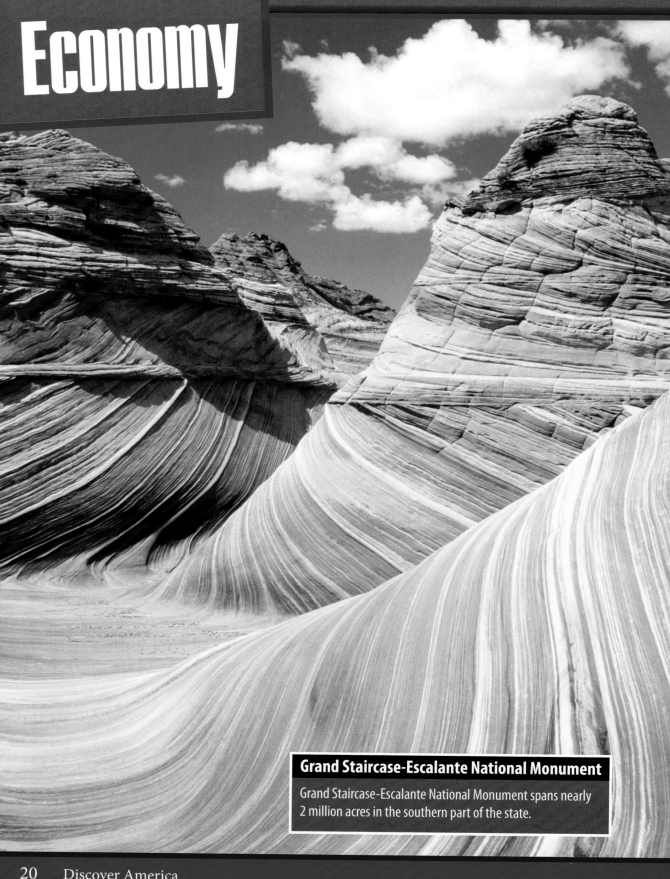

Economy

Grand Staircase-Escalante National Monument

Grand Staircase-Escalante National Monument spans nearly 2 million acres in the southern part of the state.

Tourism

Tourism is a major industry in Utah. People come from all over the world to experience the state's historic sites and natural areas. Summer is the most popular tourist season. Tourists with a taste for daring activities can try river rafting on Utah's rushing waters, as well as rock climbing and mountain biking. In the winter, visitors ski and snowboard at Utah's many ski resorts.

Tourists who visit Arches National Park can ramble around more than 2,000 natural stone arches. Salt Lake City is a popular tourist destination. Temple Square is the most visited site in the city. Brigham Young, an important Mormon leader, selected this location in 1847 for the new settlement's Mormon temple.

Bryce Canyon National Park

Bryce Canyon National Park covers more than 37,277 acres in southwestern Utah. The park is famous for the spectacular views created by its brightly colored rocks.

Temple Square

Salt Lake Temple, the largest and best-known Mormon temple in the world, is in Temple Square in Salt Lake City. More than 3 million people visit Temple Square every year.

Dinosaur National Monument

Visitors to Dinosaur National Monument can watch **paleontologists** digging for dinosaur bones. They can also learn how fossils are cleaned and preserved.

Utah's high elevation and cold winters made it the perfect spot for the 2002 Olympic Winter Games. The Olympics brought in millions of dollars of revenue to the state.

Primary Industries

Traditionally, agriculture and mining were important industries in Utah. Today, manufacturing, transportation, finance, and other service industries, including tourism, employ many more Utahans than the traditional industries do. Many people in Utah hold seasonal jobs in the tourism industry. In the winter, they may work at ski resorts or hotels that cater to skiers and snowboarders.

Many of Utah's workers are employed in service industries. The many different kinds of service jobs include waiting on tables in restaurants and repairing computers. Other Utahans work in the retail or **wholesale** businesses. Intermountain Health Care, a large chain of hospitals and other health-care facilities, has its headquarters in Salt Lake City. More than 20,000 of Utah's workers were employed by the company as of 2009, making it the state's largest employer.

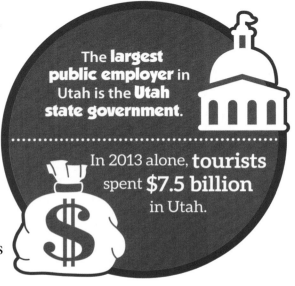

The **largest public employer** in Utah is the **Utah state government.**

In 2013 alone, **tourists** spent **$7.5 billion** in Utah.

Value of Goods and Services
(in Millions of Dollars)

Utah has many different kinds of industries. Service industries provide assistance or services to other people. One of the state's largest employers is a health-care company, which is part of the service industry. What are some services provided by people who work in health care?

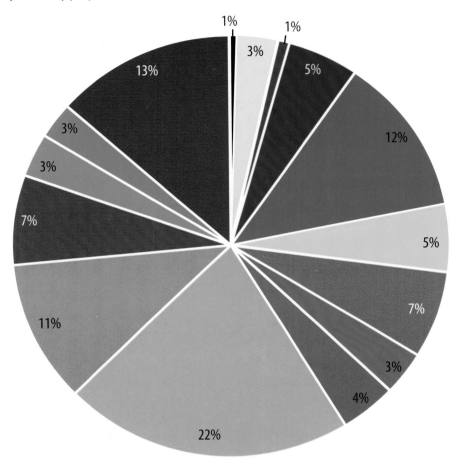

● Agriculture, Forestry, and Fishing....................$994	● Information..$5,670
● Mining $4,329	● Finance, Insurance, and Real Estate $30,169
● Utilities $1,219	● Professional and Business Services $14,979
● Construction $7,368	● Education, Health and Social Services............$9,692
● Manufacturing..................................$17,081	● Recreation and Accommodation $4,676
● Wholesale Trade................................$7,145	● Other Services...$4,100
● Retail Trade $9,562	● Government...$18,350
● Transportation and Warehousing $4,696	

Goods and Services

Utah has a diverse economy. Mining, farming, manufacturing, and tourism are the state's main economic activities. Utah's agricultural industry provides many important goods. Hay is grown to feed livestock. Wheat is grown in the northern parts of the state. Vegetables and fruits, such as potatoes, cherries, peaches, apples, and onions, are grown on irrigated farmland. Greenhouse and nursery products are also produced in Utah.

More than three-quarters of Utah's farm income is obtained from animals. The most common livestock products in Utah are beef, lamb, and dairy products. **Poultry** products, especially turkeys and eggs, are also valuable goods in the state.

Greenhouses provide controlled environments that allow many different types of plants to grow. The structures shelter plants from outside weather conditions, offering regulated heat and water.

Many different products are manufactured in Utah, including computers and office equipment. Many types of transportation equipment, ranging from space vehicles to automobile parts, are also manufactured in the state. The chemical industry, which produces medicines, and the food processing industry are very important in Utah. Other products made in the state include medical tools, fabricated metals, and paper goods.

Soda giant Coca-Cola operates a bottling plant in West Valley City, Utah.

Most of Utah's electricity is generated by steam-driven power plants, which are fueled by low-sulfur coal. Increased coal production in the Colorado Plateau has helped increase the state's mining revenues. Utah also obtains some of its power from hydroelectric plants, which convert the power of moving water into electricity.

Metal fabrication, especially steel, is an important market in Utah's manufacturing industry.

Paleo-Indian cultures were highly nomadic. These early people followed various herds as the animals moved to different grazing sites.

The Great Gallery in Horseshoe Canyon, Utah, features many pictographs, or early symbolic wall art. Scientists believe the gallery was painted by a people known as the Desert Archaic culture.

Native Americans

The first people to live in the area that is now Utah were **Paleo-Indians**. It is believed that these people lived in the region from 9,000 to 5,000 BC. These ancient people hunted large animals for food. Later, as the Paleo-Indians learned how to make more advanced hunting weapons, they began to stay in one area rather than follow the animals they hunted. They lived in caves and shelters made from wood and rocks, and they gathered plants and berries for food.

About 2,000 years ago, two different groups of Native Americans, the Ancestral Puebloan people and the Fremont, lived in the Utah area. The Ancestral Puebloan people lived in southern Utah. They grew corn, squash, and beans and raised turkeys. The Ancestral Puebloan people lived in rock dwellings built into cliffs and canyons. They are known today for the art they carved into, and painted on, the cliffs. The Fremont lived in northern Utah and were hunter-gatherers.

By the 1300s, Utah was home to several major groups of Native Americans. These groups included the Ute, the Paiute, the Shoshoni, the Goshute, and the Navajo. The largest group was the Ute, who occupied eastern Utah. By the 1800s, they lived in tepees and hunted bison, or buffalo.

Exploring the Land

In 1776, a group of explorers led by two Franciscan priests, Francisco Atanasio Domínguez and Silvestre Vélez de Escalante, entered Utah. The Domínguez-Escalante **expedition** was searching for a route from New Mexico to California. The arrival of winter forced the group to return to Santa Fe, New Mexico. Over the next few decades, merchants from Santa Fe traded goods with the Native Americans in what is now Utah.

Timeline of Settlement

1778 Don Bernardo Miera y Pacheco, a member of the Domínguez-Escalante expedition, draws the first map of Utah.

Further Exploration

1821 After winning independence from Spain, Mexico claims all of what is now Utah.

1776 The Domínguez-Escalante expedition explores the region.

1824 Jim Bridger is the first person of European descent to reach the Great Salt Lake.

1765 Spanish explorer Juan Maria de Rivera is the first European known to have visited Utah.

1827 Jedediah S. Smith becomes the first person of European descent to cross Utah from north to south and then from west to east.

Early Exploration

In the early 1800s, fur trappers and traders called mountain men explored the region while trapping beavers, minks, and other animals with valuable **pelts**. Every spring, the trappers met for an annual gathering, called a rendezvous. There, the trappers bought supplies and traded pelts with Native Americans and company agents. They also celebrated the year's success with eating, singing, and contests.

Statehood

1848 Most of the Southwest, including Utah, is transferred from Mexico to the United States at the end of the Mexican-American War.

1850 The U.S. government establishes the Utah Territory, which originally includes parts of Nevada, Colorado, and Wyoming, as well as present-day Utah.

1847 Led by Brigham Young, Mormon settlers arrive in Salt Lake Valley.

1896 Utah, with its present boundaries, becomes the 45th state on January 4.

1846 The Donner-Reed expedition travels through Utah on its way to California. Dozens of members of the party die during the journey when they are trapped by harsh winter weather.

Travelers and Settlers

It was on his second expedition west that John C. Frémont passed north of the Great Salt Lake. He followed the Snake River on his way to California.

The First Settlers

The U.S. government sent people to explore and settle the Utah area. In 1843, John Charles Frémont, a government explorer, visited the Great Salt Lake area. He returned to the region in 1845. Frémont mapped trails in Utah and described the plant and animal life he encountered in the Great Basin.

Led by Brigham Young, many Mormons left Nauvoo, Illinois, after their founder, Joseph Smith, Jr., was murdered. The first group of Mormons, including 143 men, three women, and two children, reached the Great Salt Lake valley after a 1,000-mile journey on July 21, 1847. The Mormons believed Utah was the place to create their own Zion, or kingdom of God.

The Mormons began to plow and irrigate the land on the day they arrived. They worked the land and built settlements. Spreading out, they created new settlements in neighboring areas. By 1860, about 40,000 Mormons had built more than 150 independent communities.

When Brigham Young and his fellow settlers arrived in Utah, conflicts with Native Americans were few. However, as more and more settlers arrived, disagreements over land and resources arose.

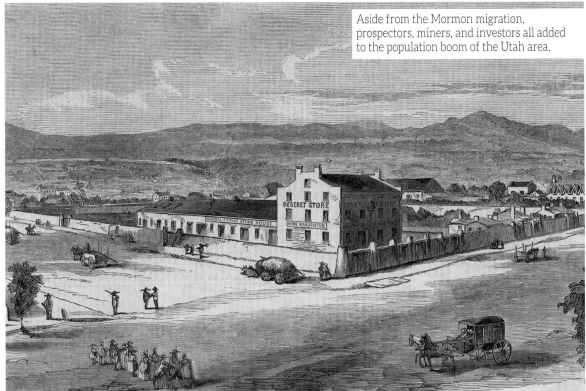

Aside from the Mormon migration, prospectors, miners, and investors all added to the population boom of the Utah area.

History Makers

Many notable Utahans contributed to the development of their state and country. They include pioneering settlers, scientists and inventors, business leaders, judges, and government officials. Well-known people born in Utah even include one of the most notorious outlaws of the Old West.

Brigham Young (1801–1877)

Born in Vermont, Brigham Young had been a Methodist but converted to Mormonism in 1832. After Mormon leader Joseph Smith, Jr. was killed, Young took over as president of the church. He wanted to find a place where his people would be free from religious persecution. He moved them to Utah, which at the time was not part of the United States. After what is now Utah became U.S. land, Young served as the Utah Territory's first governor. He is considered the founder of Salt Lake City.

Butch Cassidy (1866–1908)

Butch Cassidy, born Robert LeRoy Parker, is one of the best-known criminals in U.S. history. He was born into a Mormon family in Beaver. As an adult, Cassidy fell in with a sidekick named Harry Longabaugh, nicknamed the Sundance Kid, and a group called the Wild Bunch Gang. Together, they organized the longest successful string of train and bank robberies in the history of the American West.

Reva Beck Bosone (1895–1983)

Born in American Fork, Reva Beck Bosone taught high school before becoming a lawyer. In 1936, she was elected as a judge in Salt Lake City. Several years later, she became the first woman from Utah to be elected to the U.S. Congress, serving from 1949 to 1953. During her time in Congress, Bosone was an advocate for women and Native Americans.

Brent Scowcroft (1925–)

Scowcroft was born in Ogden and attended the United States Military Academy at West Point. He is the founder of The Forum for International Policy as well as a consulting firm. In the 1970s, and again in the late 1980s and early 1990s, he served as U.S. national security adviser, first under President Gerald Ford and then under President George H. W. Bush.

J. Craig Venter (1946–)

J. Craig Venter is a scientist who was born in Salt Lake City. He received his PhD at the University of California in San Diego and went on to create a system for tagging genes called "express sequencing tags." J. Craig Venter is responsible for sequencing the entire human genome.

Culture

Brigham Young University is a Mormon university in Utah. In 2016, there were 29,672 students enrolled.

Of the population in Utah, 30.7 percent is under 18 years old. Those who are 65 or older account for only 9 percent of the population.

The People Today

More than 2.7 million people live in Utah. A sizable majority of Utahans, more than 90 percent, are Caucasian. About 12 percent of people who live in Utah claim Hispanic or Latino roots. More than 75 percent of Utah's residents live along the Wasatch Front, which is a series of valleys and plateaus running along the Wasatch Mountains. Highly populated cities in this area include Salt Lake City, Provo, West Valley City, Sandy, Orem, and Ogden.

Utah has an excellent education system. Utah has an excellent education system, with a high **literacy** rate. In addition, some 88 percent of all Utahans graduate from high school. Utah has a very young population. Nearly one-third of its citizens are under the age of 18. People in this age group make up less than one-quarter of the U.S. population as a whole.

Utah's population **increased** by more than **500,000** people from 2000 to 2010.

Q What are some of the reasons people are moving to Utah from other states and countries?

The Utah state capitol was built in the Neoclassical style, recalling ancient Greek and Roman architecture. In 1978, it was placed on the National Register of Historic Places.

State Government

The Utah state government is divided into three branches. The governor is the head of the executive branch, which also includes the lieutenant governor, treasurer, auditor, and attorney general. Each of these officials is elected to a four-year term.

The legislative branch creates state laws. The Utah legislature includes two chambers, or parts, the Senate and the House of Representatives. The 29 senators serve four-year terms, while the 75 representatives serve two-year terms. The judicial branch of government includes the Supreme Court and eight district courts.

Like all states, Utah is represented in the U.S. Congress in Washington, D.C. Each state elects two U.S. senators, who serve six-year terms. The number of people a state sends to the U.S. House of Representatives is determined by population. Since Utah's population has been growing so rapidly, in 2013 the state increased its number of representatives to four. This is one more than it had in the previous 10 years. U.S. representatives serve two-year terms.

A 2004 restoration of the capitol building restored the House of Representatives chamber to its original colors and historical carpet.

Before becoming governor in 2009, Gary Herbert served as Utah's lieutenant governor and in the Utah Army National Guard.

Utah's state song is
"Utah, This is the Place."

*Utah! People working together
Utah! What a great place to be.
Blessed from Heaven above.
It's the land that we love.
This is the place!
Utah! With its mountain and valleys.
Utah! With its canyons and streams.
You can go anywhere.
But there's none that compare.
This is the place!
It was Brigham Young
who led the pioneers across the plains.
They suffered with the trials
they had to face.
With faith they kept on going
'till they reached the Great Salt Lake
Here they heard the words . . .
"This is the place!"*

* excerpted

This is the Place Heritage Park is located on the site where Brigham Young first spied Great Salt Lake. Several monuments commemorate the event, and the nearby Heritage Village offers visitors a look at traditional Mormon life.

Celebrating Culture

Nearly 60 percent of all Utahans are Mormon, which means that they are members of the Church of Jesus Christ of Latter-day Saints. This church was founded by Joseph Smith, Jr. in New York in 1830. The religion's beliefs are explained in *The Book of Mormon*. There are more than 13 million practicing Mormons throughout the world. The headquarters for the Church of Jesus Christ of Latter-day Saints is in Salt Lake City.

The Mormon religion places great importance on community and family life. The church community is known to help and support members through difficult times. Mormons strive to dress modestly and to avoid potentially harmful substances such as alcohol. Team sports and other athletic activities are popular with Mormons, who believe in keeping their bodies strong and healthy. The Mormon community also values education and hard work.

Five main Native American groups live in Utah. They are the Ute, the Navajo, the Paiute, the Goshute, and the Shoshoni. There are about 3,300 Ute in the state. They have their own tribal government and control about 1.3 million acres of land. There are about 7,000 Navajo, who call themselves Diné, 800 Paiute, and fewer than 500 each of the Goshute and the Shoshoni in the state.

Utah's Pioneer Day is celebrated on July 24 all around the state. Many reenactments of the Mormon pioneers' arrival to the area can be experienced throughout Utah.

November is Native American Heritage Month in Utah. Throughout the month, Native American groups gather to celebrate culture and tradition in powwows.

The Mormon Tabernacle Choir has won many awards, including one Grammy and three Emmy Awards.

Arts and Entertainment

A variety of musicians from Utah have delighted audiences across the nation. The Mormon Tabernacle Choir is a world-famous choir that began in the mid-1800s. Today, it has more than 350 singers, who make recordings as well as perform for television and radio broadcasts. Choir members are chosen for their talent and their character. Some choir members are very dedicated, traveling long distances for rehearsals, broadcasts, and other events.

The Osmonds are a well-known family from Utah. Some of the brothers began performing together in 1957. In the 1960s, the Osmond Brothers performed on a variety of popular television shows. One of the brothers, Donny Osmond, began a solo career, became a teen idol, and had numerous Top 40 hits. Donny and his sister, Marie, had their own prime-time variety show from 1976 to 1979, and their own talk show in the late 1990s. In 2016, Marie made it to the top 10 Billboard country charts once again with her single, *Music Is Medicine*.

The steam engine of the **Heber Valley Railroad** and its 10 passenger cars have made cameo appearances in more than **31 films.**

With **more than 30 major motion pictures** filmed in or nearby Kanab, Utah, the town has earned the nickname of "**Utah's Little Hollywood.**"

Various festivals are celebrated each year throughout Utah. The Utah Shakespeare Festival, founded in 1961, is held annually in Cedar City. As well as staging four Shakespeare plays every year, the festival has free "Green Shows" before each evening performance. Green Shows feature puppet shows, strolling vendors, musicians, and dancers.

The Osmond family has sold more than 102 million records worldwide.

The Festival of the American West is held in Wellsville during the last weekend of July. The fair gives visitors a taste of the Old West, with arts and crafts displays, a cowboy poetry contest, and outdoor performances featuring hundreds of entertainers. People can even witness a re-creation of a rendezvous, with participants dressed up as mountain men.

In the summertime, the Utah Shakespeare Festival puts on free Green Shows before evening performances. The Green Shows often include actors with minor roles in any of the six main productions, offering them the chance for more stage time.

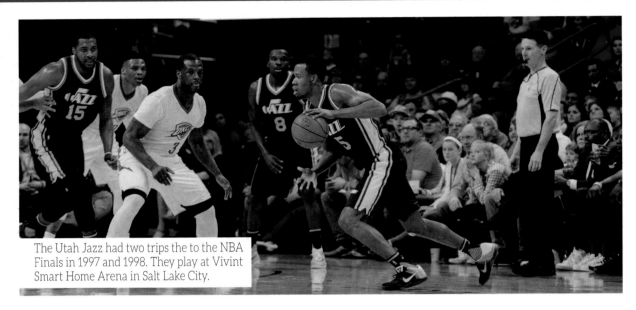

The Utah Jazz had two trips the to the NBA Finals in 1997 and 1998. They play at Vivint Smart Home Arena in Salt Lake City.

Sports and Recreation

Sports fans have many teams to cheer for in Utah. The New Orleans Jazz, which began playing in 1974, moved to Salt Lake City in 1979 to become the Utah Jazz. The Utah Jazz plays in the National Basketball Association (NBA). Collegiate sports, especially football, are popular in Utah. An intense rivalry exists between the University of Utah Utes and the Brigham Young University Cougars. The Cougar football team, led by legendary coach LaVell Edwards, won the national championship in 1984.

Utah's national parks and forests, as well as its mountain ranges, lakes, and rivers, are ideal for many types of recreational activities. Popular outdoor activities in Utah include camping, hunting, fishing, hiking, and horseback riding. Skiing and other winter sports are also enjoyed in the state. Utah has many ski resorts, including Park City, The Canyons, Alta, and Deer Valley.

The **2002 Olympics**, held in Salt Lake City, was the fifth Olympics hosted in the United States. More than **2 billion people** tuned in to watch the events.

Skiing alone accounts for **20,000 jobs** and generates **$1.29 billion** for the Utah economy.

Salt Lake City hosted the 2002 Olympic Winter Games, which were held in February. Top athletes from around the world competed in a variety of winter sports. These include ski jumping, snowboarding, bobsled, luge, figure skating, and curling.

The venues created for the Olympics are still in use. Children can take part in the Olympic experience through youth sports programs. These programs allow children to participate in and learn about an Olympic sport. The venues are also used for training and development of current and future world-class athletes. Recreational athletes may take advantage of the Olympic facilities as well.

Zion National Park offers hikers miles of trails and many scenic views of canyons, plateaus, and desert wildlife.

The United States won 34 medals at the 2002 Olympic Winter Games in Salt Lake City.

Get To Know
UTAH

During World War II, **Alta Ski** area in Park City, Utah, was used as a **paratrooper** training ground.

Utah has the highest
literacy rate
in the country.

IN UTAH, AS THE LAW STATES, BIRDS HAVE THE RIGHT OF WAY ON ALL HIGHWAYS.

Utah gave women the right to vote in 1870, 50 years before the right was granted nationwide.

PHILO T. FARNSWORTH, THE **INVENTOR OF THE TELEVISION**, WAS BORN IN BEAVER, UTAH.

THE GREAT SALT LAKE IS LARGER THAN THE STATE OF DELAWARE.

Every day, 2.6 billion gallons of water evaporate from the Great Salt Lake.

Brain Teasers

What have you learned about Utah after reading this book? Test your knowledge by answering these questions. All of the information can be found in the text you just read. The answers are provided below for easy reference.

1 Which other states join Utah at the four corners?

2 What year did Utah join the Union?

3 What are the three land regions that make up Utah?

4 Utah is the leading producer of which mineral?

5 How many types of plants are in Zion National Park?

6 What year was the first map of Utah drawn?

7 Which religious group were the first settlers of Utah?

8 In which year did Salt Lake City host the Winter Olympics?

Key Words

annuals: plants that live through only one growing season

birds of prey: birds, such as eagles and hawks, that catch and eat other animals

coniferous: trees or shrubs bearing cones and evergreen leaves

diverse: made up of many different elements

endangered: under threat of dying out

expedition: a journey made for exploration

literacy: the ability to read and write

Paleo-Indians: prehistoric humans in the Western Hemisphere, believed to have migrated from Asia

paleontologists: people who study prehistoric life by examining early remains and fossils

pelts: skins or hides of animals with the fur still attached

persecution: unfair and cruel treatment of a person or people

poultry: birds, such as chickens, turkeys, ducks, and geese, that are raised for their meat and eggs

wholesale: the sale of a large quantity of goods, especially to retail stores

Index

Log on to www.av2books.com

AV² by Weigl brings you media enhanced books that support active learning. Go to www.av2books.com, and enter the special code found on page 2 of this book. You will gain access to enriched and enhanced content that supplements and complements this book. Content includes video, audio, weblinks, quizzes, a slide show, and activities.

AV² Online Navigation

Audio
Listen to sections of the book read aloud.

Book Pages
AV² pages directly correspond to pages in the book.

Video
Watch informative video clips.

Key Words
Study vocabulary, and complete a matching word activity.

Embedded Weblinks
Gain additional information for research.

Quizzes
Test your knowledge.

Slide Show
View images and captions, and prepare a presentation.

Try This!
Complete activities and hands-on experiments.

AV² was built to bridge the gap between print and digital. We encourage you to tell us what you like and what you want to see in the future.

Sign up to be an AV² Ambassador at www.av2books.com/ambassador.